THE EVOLUTION OF
Mammals

by Sue Bradford Edwards

Content Consultant

Jack Tseng
Assistant Professor
Department of Pathology and Anatomical Sciences
University at Buffalo

Essential Library
An Imprint of Abdo Publishing | abdobooks.com

ANIMAL EVOLUTION

abdobooks.com

Published by Abdo Publishing, a division of ABDO, PO Box 398166, Minneapolis, Minnesota 55439. Copyright © 2019 by Abdo Consulting Group, Inc. International copyrights reserved in all countries. No part of this book may be reproduced in any form without written permission from the publisher. Essential Library™ is a trademark and logo of Abdo Publishing.

Printed in the United States of America, North Mankato, Minnesota.
082018
012019

THIS BOOK CONTAINS RECYCLED MATERIALS

Cover Photo: Vaganundo Che/Shutterstock Images
Interior Photos: Sun zifa/Imaginechina/AP Images, 4–5; Shutterstock Images, 6, 13, 61, 76; JonathanC Photography/Shutterstock Images, 11; Yann Hubert/Shutterstock Images, 14; Vicki Cain/Shutterstock Images, 16; DeAgostini/Getty Images, 19, 85; Christian Darkin/Science Source, 20; Flavio Vallenari/iStockphoto, 23; Dave Watts/Science Source, 24; Bob Tokyo Harris/iStockphoto, 28–29; Craig RJD/iStockphoto, 30; Anthony Smith Images/Shutterstock Images, 33; Jaime Chirinos/Science Source, 35; Millard H. Sharp/Science Source, 38–39, 71; Richard Seeley/Shutterstock Images, 42; Steve Gorton/Dorling Kindersley/Science Source, 44; iStockphoto, 46, 64, 65, 68–69, 73; Tom McHugh/Science Source, 48–49; The Natural History Museum, London/Science Source, 54; Wendy Cotie/Shutterstock Images, 58–59; Yann Hubert/iStockphoto, 78–79; Ignacio Salaverria/Shutterstock Images, 80; Khaled Desouki/AFP/Getty Images, 82; Patrick Landmann/Science Source, 88–89; Javier Trueba/MSF/Science Source, 91; Lawrence Jackson/AP Images, 93; Phil Degginger/Carnegie Museum/Science Source, 94; Dennis Kunkel Microscopy/Science Source, 95; James King-Holmes/Science Source, 98

Editor: Marie Pearson
Series Designer: Becky Daum

Library of Congress Control Number: 2018947969

Publisher's Cataloging-in-Publication Data

Names: Edwards, Sue Bradford, author.
Title: The evolution of mammals / by Sue Bradford Edwards.
Description: Minneapolis, Minnesota : Abdo Publishing, 2019 | Series: Animal evolution | Includes online resources and index.
Identifiers: ISBN 9781532116667 (lib. bdg.) | ISBN 9781532159503 (ebook)
Subjects: LCSH: Mammals--Evolution--Juvenile literature. | Animal evolution--Juvenile literature. | Biological evolution--Juvenile literature. | Mammals--Juvenile literature.
Classification: DDC 574.30--dc23

CONTENTS

A computer-generated depiction of *Juramaia sinensis* shows how the creature may have moved.

CHAPTER ONE

Jurassic Mother from China

One hundred and sixty million years ago (MYA), a tiny animal moved through the treetops. Its front paws grasped the branches as it searched for food. Worms became quick snacks. With its sharp teeth, the small, furry animal now called *Juramaia sinensis* cracked the exoskeletons of insects and ate them.

This was the late part of the Jurassic period (201.3–145 MYA). In some regions, large plant-eating dinosaurs (like brachiosaurs) and

A kangaroo joey continues to use its mother's pouch to feed after it is able to walk.

meat-eating dinosaurs (such as allosaurs) dominated the landscape. *Archaeopteryx*, a bird that had teeth and a long tail, flew through the air.

At night, in the cover of the trees, the tiny *J. sinensis* could hide from predators and seek its own prey. *Juramaia sinensis,* which means "Jurassic mother from China," is the name scientists gave this animal. It weighed less than 0.5 ounces (15 g).[1] Its skull was 0.87 inches (22 mm) long.[2] It looked like a shrew and could climb into the trees. *Juramaia sinensis* was also a placental mammal.

Scientists know that placental mammals, often called eutherian mammals, and today's marsupials evolved from a common ancestor. Marsupials are mammals that give birth to immature young that often shelter and feed in the mother's pouch. Kangaroos and opossums are marsupials. Placental mammals have a longer period of growth in the womb, so they give birth to more mature young. These young receive nutrients in the womb through a complex organ called the placenta. Dogs, horses, and human beings are placental mammals.

The *J. sinensis* specimen is the oldest known fossil of a placental mammal. It was discovered in China's Liaoning province in 2011. The fossil consists of only a partial skull and skeleton in addition to impressions of soft tissue, including hair, in the surrounding rock. This fossil is evidence that placental mammals and marsupials split apart in their evolution more than 160 MYA.

Before discovering *J. sinensis*, scientists had estimated when this split occurred. They did this by comparing marsupial DNA and placental mammal DNA based on the molecular clock hypothesis. The molecular clock hypothesis says that the order of proteins and the DNA sequences that they make up evolve at a constant rate that is unchanged over time and between organisms. Scientists compare DNA samples from two or more organisms. Based on the number of differences, they can estimate how long ago the organisms shared a common ancestor. The comparison between marsupial and placental mammal DNA suggested that the split had occurred approximately 160 MYA, but there were no fossils old enough to support this date. The previous oldest known placental mammal fossil was from 125 MYA. The discovery of *J. sinensis* helped confirm when these two mammalian branches diverged, or split into two distinct groups. Understanding how this took place requires a basic understanding of evolution.

EVOLUTION

When scientists speak of biological evolution, they are talking about the physical changes that take place in animal populations and species over time. Evolution doesn't mean a group of animals is getting better, but it doesn't mean the group is getting worse, either. It simply means a plant or animal species is changing, often in response to its environment.

One of the first people to try to explain how species change over time was French naturalist Jean-Baptiste Lamarck. In 1809, he theorized that animals could gain a trait over a lifetime and pass it down to their offspring. He used giraffes as an example, explaining that giraffes reach up to feed on tree leaves, stretching their necks and front legs. Their necks and front legs got longer, and these traits were passed down to their offspring. It didn't take long for his fellow

FOSSILIZATION

Fossilization is a process through which a plant or animal (or an animal's tracks) is preserved after it dies. Certain conditions must be met for fossilization to take place, although it can occur in several different ways. Sometimes water buries a plant or animal in sediment, such as sand, silt, or gravel. That is when the most common form of fossilization, called petrification, can occur. Buried soft tissues decay, but the bone is left behind. Water carrying minerals seeps into the bones and deposits the minerals, which crystallize. Then the bones harden along with the sedimentary rock. In another process called an external mold, when an organism completely dissolves, it can leave a space shaped just like itself in the sediment. When this shape fills with another mineral, a cast is formed. A similar process makes what is known as an internal mold. This is created when minerals fill the inside of a skull or shell and the remains then dissolve.

scientists to disprove this theory, since they could observe that large muscles from hard work and exercise are not passed on to offspring.

In 1858, Englishmen Charles Darwin and Alfred Russel Wallace independently proposed the theory of evolution through natural selection. In their theory, survival and reproduction were the mechanisms through which change occurred. Darwin explained that individuals within a species could have a number of diverse traits. These traits would make some animals faster or better able to blend in with the landscape than others. The animals with beneficial traits for their environment would survive longer and, perhaps because of this, have more offspring. Many of these offspring would inherit the beneficial traits, survive, reproduce, and pass the traits on to their own offspring. As this happened through several generations, the positive traits would be present in more individuals and the less beneficial traits would slowly disappear. As certain traits became more common and others died out, the species evolved. Darwin understood that these changes happened, but he did not know exactly how. It would take Gregor Mendel's discovery of heredity in 1866 to explain how these changes took place. Scientists later learned that heredity is caused by genes in DNA. Genes are the information encoded in DNA. They pass from parent to offspring. They determine traits, such as what color an animal's fur is or how much muscle it can build. Scientists eventually realized that

According to Darwin's theory, traits such as cheetahs' speed helped them survive and pass on those traits to offspring.

change could happen as the result of a mutation. A mutation is when the structure of a gene is accidentally changed because proteins or other molecules are substituted for others during reproduction. A beneficial mutation could assure better success in survival and reproduction and slowly spread through the population. Bad mutations make the animal more likely to die early and less likely to reproduce.

Over millions of years, descendants of relatives of *J. sinensis* evolved into human beings, cats, and even whales. If a new trait develops throughout an entire species, the species as a whole evolves. Sometimes the populations of a species are divided into two or more geographically separated groups. This might happen when the sea level rises and floods a land bridge. Or a river might cut a new channel, creating an island on which part of the species lives. Groups that are separated cannot interbreed. Because of this, one group will change in one way while another changes in another way. Eventually, the two groups will be so changed that they will become different species. This process is how the ancestral mammals similar to *J. sinensis* eventually evolved into the more than 6,000 species of modern mammals.[3]

MAMMALS DEFINED

Mammals are animals that share certain features. First, they can maintain stable body temperatures internally, unlike reptiles. A reptile must rely on a cool burrow to lower its temperature on a sunny day. If it is too cold, a reptile has to find a patch of sunlight or other warm place to raise its temperature. Mammals' bodies maintain a nearly constant temperature with the help of the hypothalamus, a gland in the brain. Nerve impulses from the skin as well as blood travel to the hypothalamus. When the blood temperature or nerve impulses show that the animal is overheating, the animal pants or sweats. Water evaporates and the mammal cools off. A mammal that is too cold can shiver to warm up. Goose bumps slow air flowing across the skin, reducing heat loss. Both cooling off and heating up use a lot of energy.

Mammals get their name from a set of organs called mammary glands. When a female mammal gives birth, mammary glands produce milk made up of water, carbohydrates, fats, protein, minerals, and disease-fighting antibodies. Young mammals nurse, feeding on this milk.

Most young mammals are born live. They don't hatch from eggs. The exceptions to this are monotremes, which include platypuses and echidnas. Monotremes lay eggs. Marsupials and placental mammals bear live young.

CLASSIFICATION

Red Fox
Vulpes vulpes

DOMAIN	**Eukaryota**. This domain includes plants, animals, and fungi. These organisms are grouped together because their cells each have a nucleus, a cell structure that contains the DNA.
KINGDOM	**Animalia**. All animals, including mammals and insects, are in this group.
PHYLUM	**Chordata**. Organisms in this phylum have a nerve cord down their backs supported by a rod of cartilage at some point in life. All animals with spines, including mammals and fish, are in this group.
CLASS	**Mammalia**. This includes all mammals, from cats and dogs to people and whales, that nurse their young.
ORDER	**Carnivora**. These animals typically eat meat and have teeth specialized for this purpose.
FAMILY	**Canidae**. This group of generally medium-sized, omnivorous animals includes wolves, dogs, foxes, and jackals.
GENUS	***Vulpes***. This genus includes foxes such as red foxes, Arctic foxes, and fennec foxes.
SPECIES	***vulpes***. Red foxes are the largest species of fox.

Taxonomic classification is the science of identifying living things, grouping them together, and naming them. When this is done, each organism is assigned a place in eight different categories ranging from domain, the most general category, to species, the most specific category. When the scientific name of an animal is given, it includes the genus, which is capitalized, and the species, which is not. Red foxes are *Vulpes vulpes*. Scientific names are often abbreviated after first use: *V. vulpes*.

WHALE HAIR

Like other mammals, whales and dolphins have hair for at least part of their lives. Before birth, baby dolphins have whiskers along their snouts. After the baby is born, the hairs fall out, but the hair follicles and the roots of the hair remain. Unlike dolphins, humpback whales (pictured) have hair throughout their lives. These hairs grow from fist-sized follicles arranged across the whale's rostrum, a form of snout. Some scientists believe the whale uses these whiskers and follicles to sense water temperature and quality. Other scientists believe whales use the whiskers to detect other animals moving through the water.

At some point during their life cycles, all mammals have hair. Hair grows out of hair follicles. Some follicles also contain nerve endings, which help mammals sense their surroundings. For example, a cat's whiskers help it feel nearby objects in the dark. A coat of hair also helps keep mammals warm and protects them from sun, bad weather, and bugs.

Other mammal traits center on the skull. Mammals have a unique lower jaw. It is a pair of bones (a bone on each side that have fused together at the chin) that moves on hinge-like joints. This combination gives mammals a strong bite and efficient chewing. Located behind and above this jaw is the mammalian ear. Unlike other animals, mammals have three tiny bones inside each middle ear space. The stirrup, anvil, and hammer were once part of the jaw, but over time they evolved into part of the middle ear. They transmit and increase sound waves, making sounds easier to hear. The mammal ear is also surrounded by bone, which insulates the animal's hearing from the noises of chewing. These features give mammals excellent hearing.

Within the body cavity, mammals have other unique features, including the arrangement of their four-chambered hearts. Blood exits the heart by a single main artery, the aorta, which curves toward the left. This artery curves to the right in birds. All other animals have more than one major artery. Mammals also have a diaphragm. This sheet of muscle and tendon separates the heart and lungs from the liver, stomach, kidneys, intestines, and reproductive organs. The diaphragm helps mammals breathe efficiently.

Last but not least, mammals have well-developed brains. Mammals are the only animals with a neocortex, a part of the brain devoted to sensory perception, motor commands, and spatial reasoning. This is also where human beings process thought and language. This array of traits can be seen in mammals ranging from tiny mice to enormous whales and people—all of which are related to ancestors of *J. sinensis*.

Monotremes

Scientists believe that birds, reptiles, and the first mammal-like reptiles diverged approximately 280 MYA. One group of mammal-like reptiles lived in Brazil approximately 235 MYA. Although they were still reptiles, complete with scales, they had some mammal-like traits such as the ratlike shape of their skulls and teeth. The descendants of the mammal-like reptiles include all mammals. Approximately 200 MYA, the monotremes split off from the other mammals. There are currently two living monotremes, the platypus and the echidna.

Rebecca Young, a biologist at the University of Texas at Austin, says that monotremes diverged before the evolution of the placenta. "In that sense they [monotremes] are somewhere between a lizard and what we think of as a human-like placental mammal," she says.[1] Because of this, today's monotremes have both reptilian and mammalian characteristics.

Echidnas have poor eyesight but excellent senses of hearing and smell.

Like reptiles, platypuses and echidnas lay eggs. They have skulls scientists describe as reptilian. Another reptilian trait is that the male platypus is venomous. Yet like mammals, platypuses and echidnas have hair and nurse their young. But the young suckle the milk through pores in the mother's skin. Other mammals have teats that supply milk.

SKULLS

The skulls of monotremes are often described as less developed or less changed than those of other living mammals in part because of their ears. Monotremes have three middle ear bones, but these bones do not move as freely as those of marsupials or other mammals. In addition, in placental mammals, a wall of bone shields the ear from the rest of the skull. In the echidna, only a bony ridge separates this middle ear from the rest of the skull, while the area is completely open in the platypus. Because their ears have not evolved the same features as those of other mammals, scientists sometimes call monotreme skulls primitive or reptilian.

FOSSIL GAPS

Little is known about the earliest monotremes, in part because relatively few fossils have been found. In addition, each fossil scientists have found represents only a small part of any single skeleton. The oldest monotreme fossil, from the early part of the Cretaceous period (145–66 MYA), was found in Australia. It is a lower jaw fragment. A type of stone called opal filled the void left behind when the bone and teeth dissolved. The species that the fossil comes from, *Steropodon galmani,* had teeth

An artist's depiction of *Steropodon galmani*, *left*, shows how it might compare to a modern echidna.

similar to those of a young platypus and was approximately the size of a house cat. It would have been one of the largest mammals alive at that time.

A jaw is also all that remains of another monotreme, *Kollikodon ritchiei*. This animal lived at approximately the same time as *S. galmani*. Because two species of monotremes existed at approximately the same time, scientists believe that monotremes had at this point diversified, becoming multiple species each with distinct characteristics. Their origin lies farther back in time.

Another noteworthy fossil was a single tooth. Found in 1992 in Argentina, it is all that remains of an ancient platypus. *Asfaltomylos patagonicus* lived during the middle to late part of the Jurassic. Because of the location of this fossil, scientists believe that monotremes once lived across southern Gondwana, a supercontinent in that period.

Fossil skulls of several echidnas were also found in Australia. These animals lived in the late part of the Neogene period (23–2.6 MYA) and early part of the Quaternary period (2.6 MYA–present). One was *Zaglossus hacketti*, which lived during the Neogene. It was the largest known monotreme that ever lived, weighing 66 pounds (30 kg) and standing up to 3.3 feet (1 m) tall.[2] With so few fossils to work with, scientists have more questions than answers about the evolution of monotremes. It is clear that in the past, these animals were more diverse in size and lived over a larger geographic area than they do today.

PANGAEA

Three hundred MYA, Earth didn't have multiple continents. There was one large landmass that scientists now call Pangaea. As the Earth shifted, Pangaea split into multiple landmasses. Approximately 200 MYA, the landmasses had shifted into two continents—Laurasia, which included modern North America, Europe, and Asia; and Gondwana, which contained South America, Africa, Australia, Antarctica, the Arabian Peninsula, and the Indian subcontinent. The land continued to shift, creating the current continents. These continents have been in position for less than 65 million years.

SURVIVAL

Although modern monotremes have evolved to fit the niches in which they live, their ranges are relatively small. The platypus lives only in eastern Australia in areas with rivers, streams, and freshwater bodies. The echidna has a somewhat broader range, living in Australia, Tasmania, and New Guinea. It lives in forested areas, on mountains, and in the desert. Monotremes were the dominant group of animals in Australia until the arrival of marsupials between 71 and 54 MYA. Given the small area in which monotremes live, some scientists wonder how they survived when competing against the more versatile marsupials.

Matthew Phillips, an evolutionary biologist at the Australian National University in Canberra, believes that monotremes moved into niches where marsupials could not follow. He thinks monotremes moved into the water. Marsupials must generally avoid water because of their young. For several weeks after a marsupial is born, it must continually suckle milk. It attaches itself to a teat and doesn't let go that entire time. If a marsupial mother were in the water for long, the young could drown.

Platypuses today are aquatic. They swim and hunt for food in the water. Echidnas, on the other hand, are terrestrial, living their entire lives on land. Recent genetic studies show echidnas and platypuses diverged between 48 and 19 MYA.

Milk

Scientists have had difficulty researching the evolution of the mammary glands. These organs produce mammals' milk. Composed of soft tissue, mammary glands do not fossilize—or at least, such a fossil has never been found. In an attempt to learn about the evolution of milk production, researchers turned to living animals. They analyzed the genes of animals that produce milk and compared them to those of animals that do not. They studied the structure of milk glands in several animals, compared the milk, and studied how these animals reproduce.

Olav Oftedal of the Smithsonian Institution believes it wasn't mammals but their ancestors that first secreted, or gave off, milk. These animals came onto land and laid eggs. These eggs allowed air to pass through, so the eggs were at risk of drying out. Oftedal believes animals that reproduced effectively secreted water and extra nutrients that the eggs absorbed. This gave these eggs a greater chance of surviving. His theory is that eventually, these secretions evolved into something to nourish the young after they hatched and after they evolved live birth.

Mammals, including cows, feed their young with milk.

Platypuses feed on worms, insects, and other things at the bottoms of streams.

Echidnas have traits that make Phillips and other scientists think an ancestor might have been semiaquatic before its descendants returned to land. Their bodies remain streamlined, a trait that is ideal for swimming. Their hind legs are oriented toward the rear, similar to those of otters and other animals that use these legs as rudders. During their development as embryos, echidnas even have duck-like bills much like the platypus. This evidence means echidnas could have been aquatic when marsupials arrived in Australia. Scientists have yet to find a semiaquatic prehistoric echidna, but that could be because there are so few fossils.

MOVING FORWARD

Scientists can make new discoveries even without new fossils if they examine old fossils in new ways. Timothy Rowe of the University of Texas in Austin did that to settle a debate about *Teinolophos,* which lived in Australia more than 100 MYA. Some scientists believed it was a monotreme ancestor to both platypuses and echidnas. Rowe and his team of researchers wanted to find out whether it was an ancient platypus, because this would suggest the platypus and echidna had diverged more than 100 MYA.

This was important because the molecular clock had been ambiguous in dating this split. The problem was that the results varied according to which protein or gene was sampled.

This method dated the split as occurring as long ago as 80 MYA or as recently as 17 MYA. Rowe hoped to find a more precise answer.

Rowe and his colleagues worked with three *Teinolophos* skulls, including one of *Teinolophos trusleri,* and took high-resolution X-ray tomography scans of each. This process is also known as a computed tomography (CT) or computed axial tomography (CAT) scan. It is a three-dimensional X-ray. The use of very strong X-rays means that the image produced is also as detailed as if someone were looking through a microscope. When Rowe and his colleagues looked at the skull scans of *T. trusleri*, the scientists saw a canal running through the jaw. The size and shape of the canal were similar to those in a modern platypus. In modern platypuses, nerves and blood vessels run through this canal to the animal's bill. Nothing like this canal is seen in modern echidnas.

Rowe and his team were left with two questions: Could a true platypus have evolved before monotremes split into echidnas and platypuses? Or could it be that the molecular estimates were wrong?

David Wake, an evolutionary biologist from the University of California, Berkeley, suggests that Rowe and his group may be asking the wrong questions. "I'm not convinced it's a platypus," he says. "We don't know anything about all the other ancient monotremes that once existed."[3] With so few fossils, Wake believes it is hard to say which fossil goes where in the monotreme family tree. He also wonders if more than one animal could have developed this canal. If so, the canal could have developed in one animal before the split, disappeared, and then redeveloped again in the platypus after the split. There is currently too little information to know, so scientists continue to go into the field to discover more fossils.

PRIMITIVE ISN'T BAD

As the science of evolution developed, early naturalists used words such as *primitive* to describe early forms and *advanced* to describe later forms. The idea was that an animal naturally advanced from a primitive, undeveloped version to a more advanced, better version. What came later was an improvement over the earlier form. Today, many scientists avoid using the word *primitive*, but when it is used, it is with a different understanding. What is primitive simply came earlier. It isn't worse. It is just first. This can be seen in the primitive, or reptilian, shoulder found in monotremes. With this shoulder configuration, these animals are weak runners, but this shoulder has other advantages, such as strong supporting muscles. In modern monotremes, these well-developed muscles are among the factors that make echidnas such strong diggers and platypuses excellent swimmers. These traits help modern monotremes continue to thrive in the environments in which they live.

A koala joey clings to its mother's back when it grows too large for the pouch.

CHAPTER THREE

Marsupials

Two of the most well-known marsupials are the koala and the kangaroo. Today, there are more than 250 different marsupials. Only two, the Virginia and the southern opossums, live in North America. All other marsupials live in South America, Australia, New Zealand, and nearby Pacific islands.

Marsupials have evolved to occupy a wide variety of niches. In Australia, the wombat and marsupial mole are powerful diggers, burrowing into the earth to avoid predators. Terrestrial species include kangaroos and wallabies, which jump to safety. Australia's gliders soar from tree to tree in search of food. Central and South America's yapock is a semiaquatic swimmer that evolved a watertight pouch to keep its young safe when the mother is swimming.

A POUCHLESS MARSUPIAL

One of the pouchless marsupials is the numbat. Unlike many marsupials, this striped animal is diurnal, meaning it is active during the day. An endangered species, it lives in only two areas of Australia, where it feeds on termites and ants. Females have two to four young at a time but have no pouch. Instead, the young each attach themselves to a nipple along the mother's abdomen. She carries them under her body while they grow. Before they release, some young may grow so large they brush the ground.

Marsupials have several traits in common. They all give birth to underdeveloped young that resemble the embryos of other mammals. Once born, young marsupials crawl up the mother's body in search of a teat. In kangaroos, koalas, and opossums, the teats are inside a pouch. In numbats, the teats are on the mother's torso. The infant latches on, and the teat fastens to the mouth tissue of the offspring. The young stay attached for weeks or months until they have matured enough to leave the pouch.

The brains of marsupials are also different from those of placental mammals. A marsupial called the quoll has a skull the size of a domestic cat's skull. Yet the quoll has approximately one-half the brain tissue of the cat. Scientists believe this smaller brain size may be one of the reasons for limited vocalizations among marsupials. While they are not completely silent, most do not have the wide range of calls found in placental mammals. They do not make distress calls, and the young do not whimper when hungry. Mammals with these unique traits have been around for a slightly shorter time than the monotremes.

ANCIENT MARSUPIAL FOSSIL

The oldest known marsupial fossil was found in China. In 2003, a team of Chinese and American scientists published an article in the journal *Science* about *Sinodelphys szalayi*. It lived alongside dinosaurs 125 MYA in what is now China's Liaoning province. Scientists identified *S. szalayi* as a marsupial by comparing it to other marsupial fossils. Its wrists, anklebones, and molars resemble those of other early marsupials.

The *S. szalayi* find is special because the mouse-sized fossil was found in its entirety. The shale imprint shows the animal's hair and details of its feet. The fossil even includes some soft tissue. Dr. Zhe-Xi Luo, then curator of vertebrate paleontology at the Carnegie Museum of Natural History in Pittsburgh, Pennsylvania, said of fossils like it, "In the past, most mammal fossils from dinosaur times are isolated teeth. As a result, we know what they ate, but not how they moved. . . . We now have the first glimpses of how these mammals moved."[1]

Hair

All mammals, even porpoises and whales, have hair at least briefly during their lives. Hair in mammals serves as insulation, helping keep animals warm in cold weather. Hair can create camouflage in the form of stripes or spots that help an animal blend into its environment. Quills and spines are part of an animal's defense. Whiskers are sensory organs that help animals feel things around them when it is too dark to see or when something is too close to focus on. For many years, biologists believed that hair evolved from scales or feathers but could find no proof in the fossil record. In 2008, biologists from several universities in Italy and Austria identified the gene that codes for the hair protein, otherwise known as hair keratin, in mammals. They looked for this same gene in a chicken and an anole lizard. They found hair keratin genes in both of these animals. It was expressed most strongly in the anole's digits. They concluded that the gene probably plays a part in claw growth in the lizard and that it originated in the most recent common ancestor to birds, reptiles, and mammals. Hair, it seems, is most closely tied not to scales or feathers but to claws.

Whiskers are long, thick hairs. When they brush against something, nerves in the animal's skin feel the movement.

The scientists noted that *S. szalayi*'s claws are proportioned like those of modern climbing animals. The shoulders and limbs are also consistent with climbing. These adaptations suggest that this animal, as with many other small animals, found safety in the trees. The last significant thing about the fossil is its age. *Sinodelphys szalayi* is older than any previous marsupial fossil. It pushed back the age for the development of marsupial mammals by 15 million years.

RADIATING AROUND THE WORLD

Most scientists agree that marsupials evolved in what is now Asia, starting around the time of *S. szalayi*. The next-oldest fossil, 110 million years old, was found in Utah. This specimen, *Kokopellia juddi*, is known by only a partial lower jaw and a few teeth. Three other species lived in the same area during the late part of the Cretaceous.

Marsupials continued to move into new niches, but how this happened varies by location. Until sometime in the Cretaceous, South America, Antarctica, and Australia were connected as parts of the supercontinent of Gondwana. Monotremes, marsupials, and other mammals moved into what would later become three separate landmasses.

When Australia separated from the landmass, it shifted north. As it moved, the climate changed from warm and wet to dry and cold and back to warm and wet. Between 23 and

Thylacoleo is sometimes known as a marsupial lion because it resembled large cats.

15 MYA, during this second warm, wet tropical phase, giant marsupials thrived. *Diprotodon* was the largest known marsupial to ever live. This giant wombat grew up to 13 feet (4 m) long and weighed nearly 6,000 pounds (2,700 kg).[2] Another was the giant short-faced kangaroo, or *Procoptodon*, which stood 6.6 feet (2 m) tall.[3] *Thylacoleo*, a lionlike marsupial, weighed up to 350 pounds (160 kg).[4] All probably evolved from ancestors similar to tiny *S. szalayi*.

In South America, marsupials thrived in niches where they had little or no competition. One South American marsupial was *Borhyaena*. It was not related to the hyena, although it did have a similar muscled build. Discovered in 1887, this 200-pound (90 kg) predator lived during the early to middle part of the Neogene.[5] *Borhyaena* died out when another marsupial predator, *Thylacosmilus*, dominated its niche.

Thylacosmilus had massive canines much like a saber-toothed cat. But unlike the saber-toothed cat's teeth, those of *Thylacosmilus* grew throughout the animal's life. These teeth required constant wear to keep them at a manageable length. This animal was up to 3.9 feet (1.2 m) long and lived during the Neogene.[6]

WHY NOT AFRICA?

By 2018, only one marsupial fossil had been found in Africa. *Peratherium africanum* lived 23 MYA in what is now Egypt. In their book *Mesozoic Mammals*, paleontologists Jason Lillegraven, Zofia Kielan-Jaworowska, and William Clemens theorize that Africa may have had many marsupials but none of the remains fossilized. As evidence, they point out that the only fossilized mammal remains from this time period found in Africa were found in Egypt. If only one small area offered the right conditions to create fossils, a wealth of information may have been lost from the rest of the continent.

During the late part of the Neogene, an isthmus, or narrow bridge of land, opened between North America and South America. This enabled the placental mammals to migrate into South America, where they took over the majority of niches previously occupied by marsupials.

RECENT EVOLUTION

The evolution of modern marsupials is reflected in the ways their physiological, or bodily, processes have adapted to take advantage of different foods. Some have adapted to consume foods toxic to other animals. The koala is one of three marsupials that eat eucalyptus leaves. These tree leaves are difficult to digest and low in nutrition. One adaptation that allows the koala to live on a eucalyptus-leaf diet is its ability to sleep 18 to 22 hours a day.[7] This helps the koala burn fewer calories than it would if it were awake. To get the maximum nutrition from the leaves, koalas evolved a longer cecum than other mammals. This digestive organ is full of bacteria that break down the leaves. Marsupials have adapted highly specialized ways to survive in niches ranging from the eucalyptus groves of Australia to the stream banks of South America.

EUCALYPTUS FEEDERS

The koala may be the best-known eucalyptus feeder, but it is not the only one. The greater glider and the ringtail possum also eat eucalyptus leaves. The fluffy, cat-sized greater glider feeds on eucalyptus and mistletoe, another plant that is toxic to many animals. The ringtail possum eats a variety of foods including the buds off rosebushes in people's gardens and a variety of native Australian leaves, fruits, and flowers. To get the maximum nutrition from eucalyptus leaves, the ringtail possum evolved an unusual process. It eats and redigests its own feces. This helps the possum get the most nutrition from its food in two ways. Not only does it digest the same eucalyptus leaves twice but the feces also contain microorganisms that help in the digestive process.

While koalas don't eat their own feces, young koalas eat pap. When a young koala nuzzles its mother's rear, she releases several ordinary fecal pellets before releasing runnier pap, which the young koala eats. Pap is full of the mother's gut bacteria. Eating it helps the young koala digest eucalyptus once it is an adult. Animals evolve many ways to get the most out of their food.

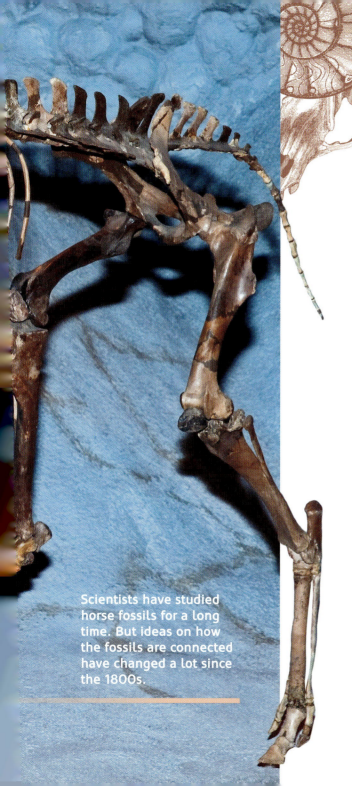

Scientists have studied horse fossils for a long time. But ideas on how the fossils are connected have changed a lot since the 1800s.

CHAPTER FOUR

The Horse

When the first discoveries on the horse's lineage were being made in 1839, paleontology was still a very young science. Few fossils had been collected and categorized, so scientists did not know where to look for new fossils. In addition, scientists at that time had no understanding of evolution as a slow, gradual process.

By the 1870s, many horse fossils had been found. One of the scientists examining these finds was T. H. Huxley. Huxley was a big advocate for Darwin's theory of evolution by natural selection. In fact, he so passionately defended the theory that he called himself Darwin's Bulldog. Huxley observed the changes in horse fossils found in higher layers of rock in a fossil bed compared to those in lower layers. Huxley discussed the idea that species changed slowly and gradually.

WHO'S WHO IN EARLY PALEONTOLOGY

Joseph Leidy is sometimes called the founder of US paleontology. He wrote the 1847 article "On the Fossil Horse of America." In this article, he showed that ancient horses had lived and become extinct in North America long before the late 1400s. In other work, Leidy found evidence that ancient lions, camels, and rhinoceroses had lived in the western United States. His fellow paleontologists respected his work. Another noteworthy paleontologist was O. C. Marsh. He became the first professor of vertebrate paleontology in the United States, working his entire career at Yale University in New Haven, Connecticut. From 1870 until his death, Marsh led expeditions almost every year to search for American fossils. He discovered at least 1,000 fossil vertebrates and described another 500, including toothed birds, gigantic horned mammals, and dinosaurs.[1] Like Leidy, he also published about prehistoric horses in the Americas. Mary Anning was a British fossil collector in the 1800s. She helped make important early discoveries and establish paleontology as a field of science.

Early in the science of paleontology, scientists such as Joseph Leidy in the 1850s and O. C. Marsh in the 1870s thought of evolution as a ladder. One ancient horse led to another, better ancient horse. The older species gave way to a better one. Today, scientists discuss family trees with many branches, some of which end or die out. They know these changes take many years to become visible. They also know that animals don't evolve to become more advanced. Animals evolve to survive and reproduce in the environments in which they live.

THE FIRST HORSE

The earliest known fossil horse is known as *Hyracotherium*. It lived 56 to 34 MYA in modern Europe and North America. The small animal stood up to two feet (60 cm) tall at the shoulders.[2] It had four toes on each front foot and three on each rear foot. Each toe ended in a heavy nail or small hoof. With long legs for its body size, *Hyracotherium* probably relied on speed to protect itself from predators. The size and shape of its teeth tell scientists that it ate leaves rather than grass.

After *Hyracotherium*, the next ancestral relative of the modern horse is *Mesohippus*, which lived from 40 to 30 MYA, overlapping with *Hyracotherium*. *Mesohippus* was approximately four feet (1.2 m) long and weighed 75 pounds (34 kg).[3] With a larger brain and elongated muzzle, the shape of the skull more closely resembled that of modern horses, but it fed on fruits and twigs in the forests of North America and had three toes on each foot.

Next in order of appearance was *Miohippus*, which lived 35 to 25 MYA. It was approximately the same size as *Mesohippus*. The *Miohippus*

DAWN HORSE

In 1839, the English paleontologist Richard Owen identified and named the earliest prehistoric horse. It was the size of a dog and had a curved spine. He thought it was related to the hyrax, a small rodent-like mammal. So he named his find *Hyracotherium*. In 1876, Marsh found and named *Eohippus*, meaning "dawn horse." A few years later, another American paleontologist, E. D. Cope, realized that *Hyracotherium* and *Eohippus* were the same animal. Scientific convention meant that even though the animal is not a hyrax, Owen's name would be the one used because he named his discovery first. Despite this, journalists and other writers continue to use the more poetic name *Eohippus*.

genus evolved in two different types. One continued to live in the forests, and the other moved out onto the plains.

Parahippus was the first premodern horse to feed on grass. It lived from 24 to 17 MYA. Grasses became widespread on the plains at that time. *Parahippus* evolved to take advantage of this source of food. It developed teeth that grew throughout its life. Eating tough grasses kept the teeth worn down to a proper length. *Parahippus* also had an elongated head and was the first ancient horse to look like a modern horse.

Modern horses are descended from *Pliohippus*, which lived from 12 to 6 MYA. It disappeared from North America 10,000 to 8,000 years ago. Scientists have many hypotheses but no solid evidence as to what the main cause was. Some say early humans hunted

TODAY'S HORSE

Although prehistoric horses evolved largely in North America, they disappeared from the continent 10,000 years ago. Wild horses in the Americas today, including mustangs (pictured), did not evolve here. They are descended from domestic European horses that came over first with Spanish explorers and later with other settlers. Some of these horses escaped or were abandoned, leading to the feral horses in the Americas today.

Pliohippus to extinction. Others believe new diseases to which these horses had no resistance developed. But before *Pliohippus* disappeared in North America, it had spread throughout South America and into Europe, Africa, and Asia. Ancient horses continued to evolve in these regions, developing the single toe or hoof they have today.

FEWER TOES

Members of the family Equidae, which includes horses, donkeys, and zebras, are the only animals that walk on one toe per foot. Because of this, scientists have worked to discover what the evolutionary advantage of this single hoof could be. How did it help them survive?

To answer this question, scientists from Harvard University used micro-CT scans to create three-dimensional models of the lower legs and feet of 12 extinct horses and a tapir. They chose the tapir because, like *Hyracotherium*, it has four toes on the front foot and three on the rear. Once the scans had been made, the researchers used them to model the stresses these bones are under when the animal jumps and runs.

The computer models showed that early horse ancestors needed the extra toes. The smaller toes on either side of the larger middle toe helped distribute the weight when the animal ran and jumped. Without the smaller toes, the larger middle toe would have fractured.

The leg and foot structure of an early horse, *left*, was very different from that of modern horses.

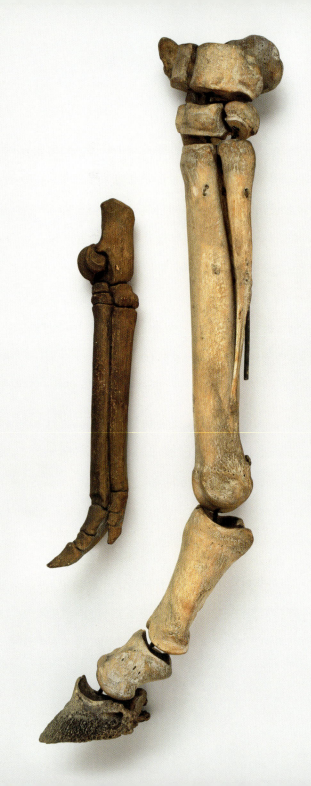

"As body mass increased, and side toes shrunk, the middle digit compensated by changing its internal geometry, allowing ever-bigger horse species to eventually stand and move on one toe," says Harvard evolutionary biologist Stephanie Pierce.[4] The bone evolved, moving off center and becoming thicker. This allowed it to resist bending and breaking when under the strain of a running, jumping animal. With this one toe, the horse could run faster over grasslands. A single toe offered another advantage as well. Fewer toes reduced the weight of the foot. This reduced the amount of energy required to pick up and move the foot, an important consideration when eating a low-energy food such as grass.

DIET FIRST

In addition to creating computer models, scientists are finding new ways to examine large numbers of fossils to test theories. Researchers know that the changing climate 20 MYA caused grasslands to spread through the areas where prehistoric horses roamed. Researchers theorized that because of this change in food, horses evolved the teeth needed to eat grass. In earlier studies, researchers examined microwear, or microscopic patterns of wear on the teeth, and chemically analyzed teeth to see what foods the animals were eating. This was a slow process, so not enough samples were screened to prove or disprove the theory.

Horses today eat grass. Their teeth continually grow to counteract how much chewing grass grinds down their teeth.

In 2005, paleo-dental researchers at the New York College of Osteopathic Medicine and

the American Museum of Natural History conducted a study of how available food sources

influenced the evolution of the horse. These scientists used the mesowear method to study diet. Mesowear examines the shape of the tooth and the sharpness of each tooth's cusps. The cusps are the bumps or points on a tooth. Canine teeth, for example, each have one cusp. The sharpness is an indicator of the wear on the tooth caused by chewing.

These scientists took data from the teeth of 6,500 individual horses from 70 extinct species. The fossil samples dated from 55 MYA to the extinction of the prehistoric horse in the Americas. Once they had analyzed the tooth wear, the researchers compared it with records of the climate change that caused a shift in vegetation from rain forests that produced fruit and leafy, woody vegetation to open grasslands. They noted that the change in tooth wear caused by grazing on grass occurred 18 MYA. This was the time when climate change led to the spread of grasslands. They concluded that the change in environment had indeed forced changes in the horse's diet, tooth wear, and eventually physiology as the horse adapted to running on the open plains.

MODERN FEED

Experts in equine nutrition emphasize that it is important to know the diet horses evolved to eat. Small changes to diet will change the physiology of the animal over time, reshaping teeth, jaws, and even the digestive system. In addition, feed that is too different from the diet that shaped the horse's evolution will cause health problems. Food with few fibers means that teeth will not wear down enough. Overlong teeth will give the horse trouble unless they are filed down by a vet or a trimming specialist called a farrier.

CHAPTER FIVE

Human Beings

When Darwin published *On the Origin of Species* in 1859, newspapers claimed that he said people descended from apes. In reality, he said humans and apes have a common ancestor. Based on genetic data, scientists believe the split between humans and other great apes occurred during the middle part of the Neogene.

Two years before Darwin's publication, German quarrymen discovered a fossil in the Neander Valley. They found a thick-boned skull with heavy brow ridges. Some scientists decided the fossil was a human ancestor or other human relative. They named it Neanderthal for the valley in which it was found, *thal* being Old German for "valley."

THE NEANDERTHALS

Neanderthals lived in Eurasia from 400,000 to 30,000 years ago, which means they lived during the Ice Age. They took shelter from the cold in the area's limestone caves. This is where many of their fossils have been found, leading to the nickname "cave men." They looked like short, muscular people with extreme cheekbones, heavy brows, and wide noses. Scientists now believe their appearance was an adaptation to the cold. Short and stocky bodies conserve heat better than tall and slender ones. Scientists are also debating whether their large noses might have been an adaptation that would have allowed them to warm and humidify cold, dry air before pulling it deep into their lungs. Making and using stone tools enabled them to hunt and prepare food. There is also evidence of them using campfires. The debate rages on about just how advanced they were, but Neanderthals adapted physically and culturally to the Ice Age environment.

Then in 1891, Dutch geologist Eugène Dubois was digging on the Indonesian island of Java. He found the top of a skull and a femur, the upper leg bone. The partial skull was too small for a human-sized brain, but the femur was shaped for humanlike, bipedal walking. Dubois shared his find publicly in 1894. Other scientists said it was the remains of an ape or a deformed human. Discouraged, Dubois hid the fossils away and did not let other scientists examine the find until 1923. At that time, they classified the fossil as *Homo erectus*, a group of human ancestors that lived 1.8 million to 143,000 years ago. Because of this find, many scientists wondered if humankind had evolved in Asia.

The following year, anthropologist Raymond Dart identified a fossil found by a group of miners in South Africa. Dart realized that the skull was that of a human ancestor and named it *Australopithecus africanus*. *Australopithecus africanus* lived from 3.3 to 2 MYA and was bipedal, but the skull, with its low slope, heavy brow, and large teeth, looked apelike. In addition, the arms and shoulders were adapted for climbing. Dart believed that it was part of the human family tree.

THE LEAKEYS

In 1931, archaeologist Louis Leakey joined the search for human fossils. Some scientists were searching in Europe. Others chose Asia. Leakey set up his search in Olduvai Gorge, Tanzania. He agreed with Dart and Darwin. The oldest human fossils would be in Africa.

Although Leakey and his team found stone tools, it wasn't until 1959 that they made their first fossil find. Archaeologist Mary Leakey, Louis Leakey's wife, spotted a piece of bone. Brushing away the soil, she found teeth. Excavation revealed the pieces of a skull, which was later named *Australopithecus boisei*. Other scientists had found *A. boisei* fossils, but it was only with the addition of Mary Leakey's find that they realized it was a new species. Scientists now know that *A. boisei* lived 2.3 to 1.2 MYA. Its heavy skull included a sagittal crest. This bony ridge on top of the skull provides an anchor for large chewing muscles needed to chew leafy foods.

This fossil was not the remains of a tool-using ancestor that the Leakeys sought.

INSPIRING OTHERS

Louis Leakey was a primatologist, one who studied primates other than modern humans. Because apes and humans are closely related, he believed that studying the behavior of wild apes could help scientists understand human ancestors. With his encouragement and support, British researcher Jane Goodall studied chimpanzees at the Gombe Stream National Park in Tanzania starting in 1960. In 1967, American primatologist Dian Fossey arrived at Virunga Volcanoes of Rwanda to study the mountain gorillas. In 1971, Canadian conservationist Biruté Galdikas settled among Borneo's orangutans. These women made the public more aware of primates and how people can keep them alive for future generations.

In 1960, the Leakeys' adult son Jonathan found a partial jaw. Paired with other fragments his parents found later, it had a larger brain and was finer boned than *A. boisei*. Louis thought it must be capable of tool use. He named this fossil *Homo habilis*, Latin for "man with skill." Scientists slowly realized that Leakey was right. *Homo habilis* was skilled and able to use tools. *Homo habilis* (2.4–1.4 MYA) was different from *Australopithecines*. In addition to having the ability to walk upright, *H. habilis* had a larger brain, and its thumbed hands could handle a tool. Still, only scientists thought of *H. habilis* and other ancestral species as human ancestors. To most people, these finds were nothing more than a bit of skull or a few teeth. That changed with one special find.

LUCY

In 1974, a team of researchers led by Donald Carl Johanson of Case Western Reserve University and Maurice Taieb of France's National Center for Scientific Research uncovered the fossil of a 20-year-old female. They had discovered much of a single three-million-year-old skeleton, allowing them to judge her height and build. That night at the campfire, they nicknamed her Lucy, after the Beatles song "Lucy in the Sky with Diamonds." Later, they realized they had found a new species, which they named *Australopithecus afarensis*.

Australopithecus afarensis lived in eastern Africa from 3.85 to 2.95 MYA. It ranged in height from thee feet five inches to four feet 11 inches (105–151 cm) and weighed from 64 to 92 pounds (29–42 kg).[1] Lucy captured the public imagination like never before. People wondered how she had lived, what she ate, and how she died. People wanted to know about their ancient past. Leakey's *H. habilis* was the first tool user discovered, but although Lucy still looked very apelike, she had a name, and that helped people care.

Scientists made a cast, or replica, of *A. afarensis*. Scientists can use a cast to study the structure of a fossil if they want to avoid possibly damaging the real fossil.

WHAT IS HUMAN?

When scientists find an early human fossil, they study it to see where it might fit into the family tree. They check how human it looks. They check for apelike features. The difference is not always clear, because a skull can include some features that are more human and others that are less human. When Leakey named *H. habilis,* some scientists felt it was too similar to *Australopithecus* for a separate classification. Although opinion has shifted, the debate continues. What traits look human?

Apelike skulls have several distinct features. One of the most obvious is the sagittal crest. Apes also have large brow ridges shadowing their eye sockets. Behind their eye sockets, the skull narrows.

Human skulls differ from ape skulls. They have only moderate brow ridges with little or no narrowing of the skull behind the eye sockets. In part, these changes occurred because of the increased skull size needed to house the larger human brain. Human ancestors, with their pronounced brow ridges and narrowed skull behind the eye sockets, fit between modern humans and apes.

The teeth and mouth also vary from ape to modern human. Apes have large, pointed canines as well as canine diastemas, which are gaps on the opposite jaw into which the canine teeth slot when the mouth is closed. Modern humans have less pronounced canines and no diastema.

In 2003, *Homo floresiensis* was discovered on the island of Flores in Indonesia. The find was dated from 100,000 to 50,000 years ago. The brain size is smaller than that of early hominids and smaller even than that of an *Australopithecus* or a chimpanzee. But *H. floresiensis* made tools. Scientists think *H. floresiensis* is descended from *H. erectus*, but that living on an island created evolutionary pressures that made members of the species smaller. With limited food available on the island, smaller individuals that did not need to eat as much gained an evolutionary advantage.

HOW DIFFERENT ARE WE?

A human skull and an ape skull look very different, but recent genetic studies have found that human DNA and chimpanzee DNA are 98.8 percent alike.[2] Humans and gorillas are 98.4 percent similar. Human, chimpanzee, and gorilla genes are 96.9 percent similar to orangutans. One human being and another normally only differ by 0.1 percent, meaning that any two people are 99.9 percent alike.[3]

KENYANTHROPUS

Another extinct human relative was discovered in 1999 when a group of researchers found a fossilized skull in West Turkana, Kenya. Approximately 3.5 million years old, it would have lived at the same times as *A. afarensis*. The face was flatter than that of *A. afarensis*. Fred Spoor of the Max Planck Institute for Evolutionary Anthropology in Germany and Meave Leakey of the Koobi Fora Research Project named it *Kenyanthropus platyops*.

Other scientists suggested *K. platyops* was simply an *A. afarensis* skull flattened by damage. In 2010, Spoor and Meave Leakey reexamined the skull with Koobi Flora's Louise Leakey. They took CT scans to see how damaged the skull was. Despite several cracks, the skull's shape was largely unaltered. After they compared *K. platyops* to *A. afarensis,* six other extinct hominid species, modern humans, chimpanzees, and gorillas, they stood by their original claim. With its small molars and flat face, *K. platyops* is a new species. Just where it fit into the evolutionary framework remained to be seen.

OUT OF AFRICA

In January 2018, a group of researchers published their findings on a jawbone fragment discovered in Misliya Cave in Israel. The fragment is the left portion of a maxilla, or upper jaw. The teeth reveal that it is *Homo sapiens*, a human.

The truly surprising part is that it dates to between 199,000 and 177,000 years ago. Before this find, scientists believed that *H. sapiens* had not left Africa until 122,000 years ago. The teeth are also more modern than East African *H. sapiens* teeth of the same period. This find may reveal the route of *H. sapiens* from Africa through Israel into Asia. But there are still many questions to be answered about human origins.

Members of Canidae have teeth specially designed for grabbing and cutting meat.

CHAPTER SIX

Dogs

Dogs are canids, belonging to the family Canidae. Canidae is one of the oldest groups of carnivores, or meat eaters. The earliest known canid is *Prohesperocyon wilsoni*, identified from a single skull and lower jaw. The fossil dates to approximately 36 MYA and was discovered near Big Bend National Park in West Texas. Even with such a small portion of the skeleton, it was identified as a canid by its teeth, which are shaped for cutting meat, and also by bone that shields its middle ear.

Modern canids include coyotes, foxes, jackals, wolves, and the many breeds of modern dogs. Coyotes can be up to 37 inches (94 cm) long and weigh up to 50 pounds (23 kg).[1] They live throughout North and Central America, from Canada to Panama, and hunt rodents, rabbits, and deer. Most species of fox are approximately one-half the size of a coyote, but the smallest, the fennec fox, is only nine inches (23 cm) long and weighs

3.3 pounds (1.5 kg).[2] Foxes live in North and South America, Europe, Asia, and North Africa

and have a varied diet depending on terrain. Jackals live throughout Africa and are generally

33 inches (85 cm) long and weigh up to 26 pounds (12 kg).[3] Unlike some of their fellow canids,

foxes and jackals eat both plants and animals. While these canids are wild and often skittish

around people, dogs have developed to live alongside humans.

DOGS AND DARWIN

Darwin was known to be a dog lover. He lived with terriers, a retriever, a Pomeranian, a

pointer, and a Scottish deerhound. As a scientist and observer, Darwin took note of the varied

appearance and temperament of dogs. Darwin concluded that the extreme variation in dogs

could only have come about if they were descended from more than one wild ancestor.

He noted:

> When we reflect on the inherent improbability of man having domesticated throughout the
>
> world one single species alone of so widely distributed, so easily tamed, and so useful a group
>
> as the Canidae; when we reflect on the extreme antiquity of different breeds; and especially
>
> when we reflect on the close similarity, both in external structures and habits, between the

Dogs come in many sizes, colors, and coat types. Darwin tried to understand how they could be so diverse.

domestic dogs of various countries and the wild species still inhabiting these same countries,

the balance of evidence is strong in favor of multiple origin of our dogs.[4]

Darwin theorized that the greyhound, with its lean build, might be descended from the Abyssinian *Canis simensis,* or Ethiopian wolf. Larger dogs, he believed, were descended from gray wolves. The smaller, less muscular dogs, according to Darwin, were the descendants of jackals. Some scientists supported the theory that different dogs evolved from different groups of wolves. Other scientists looked for a single ancestral group. Only recently have scientists begun to unravel the origins of the dogs people keep as pets.

HOW WERE DOGS TAMED?

When scientists say that dogs were domesticated, they don't mean tamed like the pets of today. The first wolves to live alongside humans simply started hanging around a camp of hunter-gatherers. Dr. Krishna Veeramah believes the wolves lived near people to scavenge for scraps of food. The wolves that acted less aggressive toward the people would have fared better, getting more food without being chased away or killed. With more food, they would have been able to feed more puppies. One scientist who demonstrated how this could have taken place was Russian geneticist Dmitri K. Belyaev. In the 1950s, he and an intern, Lyudmila Trut, visited farms where foxes were raised for their furs. They watched how the foxes behaved when the cages were opened, looking for foxes that didn't try to hide and didn't act aggressive. The two scientists bred the calmer foxes, then bred the calmest pups of those litters. The foxes were not tamed, and time spent with humans was kept to a minimum. By the fourth generation, the fox pups acted like dogs, wagging their tails and approaching the humans, simply through the scientists selecting for the calmest, friendliest animals.

MAN AND DOG

In 2013, a group of scientists sequenced the genes of four gray wolves from Russia and China, three feral dogs living in Chinese cities, and three domesticated dogs: a German shepherd, a Belgian Malinois, and a Tibetan mastiff. Street dogs are not bred by humans for certain traits. Instead, they roam city streets, hunting, scavenging, breeding, and surviving. Weiwei Zhai, a genetics researcher at Beijing's Chinese Academy of Science, and the other researchers believe these feral dogs represent a link between wolves and modern dog breeds.

Once the DNA had been sequenced, the scientists compared the canine gene sequences with those of human beings. They found that human and dog DNA had some of the same traits. These traits influence how cholesterol is processed, susceptibility for some cancers, and the transportation of serotonin, a chemical the body produces that helps regulate mood and promotes good social behavior, appetite, and sleep. The scientists who conducted this study note that all of the things serotonin regulates come into play when population density increases, as would happen with dogs and humans living together in settled communities.

The selection for the same genes in two different species is called convergent evolution. This occurs when two distantly related organisms develop the same traits independently. Zhai said that finding convergent evolution in canines and humankind wasn't surprising. He explained that it could easily have happened in dogs and in people because the two have shared the same environment for thousands of years. Whatever environmental factors selected for a trait in dogs could easily select for the same trait in humans and vice versa.

NOT THESE WOLVES

Even as one group of scientists studied how a shared environment might influence two species that live together, another group continued to try to determine when dogs and wolves diverged. In late 2013, an international team of scientists compared the DNA of dogs and wolves. The wolf samples came from three gray wolves. One wolf came from China, another

WHICH WOLF IS WHICH?

Recent genetic studies show two types of modern wolves, the larger gray wolf and the Ethiopian or Abyssinian wolf (pictured). Before genetic testing, scientists thought there were two types of American wolves, the gray wolf and the red wolf. They now know the red wolf descended from a mixing of gray wolves and coyotes. The smaller Ethiopian wolf actually looks more like a coyote than a gray wolf. It was thought to be a jackal until genetic testing proved otherwise. Appearances can be deceiving.

from Croatia, and the third from Israel. They chose these countries because scientists have discovered early dogs in all three countries, suggesting that one or more of these areas might be where dogs were first domesticated.

The scientists obtained DNA from two dogs—a basenji in central Africa and a dingo in Australia. Although dingoes are wild, some scientists consider them a subspecies of the domestic dog. The researchers selected the basenji and dingo because both are isolated from modern wolf populations. The study also used the DNA of a boxer from Europe that another group of scientists had sequenced in an earlier experiment.

Upon examining the DNA, the scientists found that the dogs were most closely related

People living near the headwaters of the Nile and Congo rivers use basenjis for hunting. The breed had little to no contact with European dogs until the late 1800s.

to each other. None were closely related to any of the wolves. The three wolves were also more closely related to each other than to any of the dogs.

This was not what the scientists expected to find. They thought that they would find one of two things. Perhaps all three dogs would be related to one wolf. Or each dog would be descended from the closest wolf population. Instead, their findings suggest that both wolves and dogs seem to have descended from an older ancestor.

WHY DOGS LOOK DIFFERENT

Phenotype is a scientific word describing how genes are expressed, meaning how an organism looks. In studying dog DNA, scientists in the CanMap project found that a dog's phenotype is governed by only a small number of genes, because people breeding dogs created what scientists call a genetic bottleneck. A bottleneck is where a pathway narrows and restricts flow. In this case, the people who founded a dog breed, such as the Irish setter, chose dogs with a very specific set of characteristics. This decision created a bottleneck, allowing only the genes of the small number of founding animals to pass to future generations. One breed got some genes from the ancestor dogs. Another breed got different genes from the ancestors.

EUROPEAN WOLVES

Scientists didn't give up on linking wolves and dogs. In 2017, a group of researchers studied the DNA of two ancient dogs found in Germany. One was 5,000 years old, and the other was 7,000 years old. The scientists were able to obtain a DNA sample from each fossil.

The gene sequence of the ancient dogs revealed that, at least at the genetic level, they were similar to dogs today. "We found that our ancient dogs from the same time period were very similar to modern European dogs, including the majority of breed dogs people keep as pets," explained Dr. Krishna Veeramah, a genetics professor at Stony Brook University in New York.[5]

These ancient dogs lived alongside Neolithic farmers in Europe, a period which lasted from 7,000 to 2,300 years ago. They were not like the pets of today but probably lived within or near the village, roaming freely and scavenging for their own food, much like modern street dogs. Although they were not tame like modern pets, they did resemble them in some ways. They had floppy ears, and their skulls were smaller than those of wolves.

The study estimated that dogs split from wolves from 40,000 to 20,000 years ago. But where were they domesticated? With 5,000- and 7,000-year-old fossils being found in Europe, Veeramah believes that that is where scientists will find the link between ancient dogs and nearby wolves. It is clear that genetic continuity between these ancient dogs shows one point of origin, not the multiple points of origin Darwin theorized.

The Siberian tiger is the largest tiger subspecies.

CHAPTER SEVEN

Cats

Thirty-seven species of cats live in the world today.[1] Native to all continents except Australia and Antarctica, they range in size from massive to petite. The tiger is up to 13 feet (4 m) long and 660 pounds (300 kg).[2] The petite rusty spotted cat is only 19 inches (48 cm) long and 3.5 pounds (1.6 kg).[3] The problem with trying to determine which prehistoric cat evolved into another is that under their fur, they all look a lot alike. Even an expert can have trouble telling the skull of a tiger from that of a lion.

One of the oldest cat ancestors is *Proailurus,* meaning "first cat." *Proailurus* lived 30 MYA and was about the size of a house cat. Although the teeth are feline and it had retractable claws, with its long, slender body it looked more like a tree-climbing mongoose than a cat. The next oldest feline ancestor is the *Pseudaelurus,* named in 1850 by French zoologist Paul Gervais. *Pseudaelurus* lived between 9 and 20 MYA. Species varied in size from house cat to cougar. The *Pseudaelurus* line split, with one branch leading to the now-extinct line of saber-toothed cats and the other leading to all modern cats living today.

FELINE DNA

In 2007, Stephen O'Brien and Warren Johnson of the Genetic Cancer Institute in Frederick, Maryland, finalized a study that used DNA to discover information about the ancestors of modern cats. They took skin samples from every species alive today, even the most elusive and most rare. Once they had sequenced the various samples, they compared a sequence of 30 genes found in each sample. From this, they could identify eight evolutionary lines and tell in which order each split off.[4] They created a feline family tree with dates for the base of each branch provided by using the molecular clock model, with the help of dated fossils as a time line.

The comparison allowed them to identify a species of *Pseudaelurus* as the closest to the ancestral lineage of all cats. *Pseudaelurus* lived in Asia approximately 11 MYA. The first line to diverge was pantherines, or roaring cats. Ancient pantherines evolved into the lion, tiger,

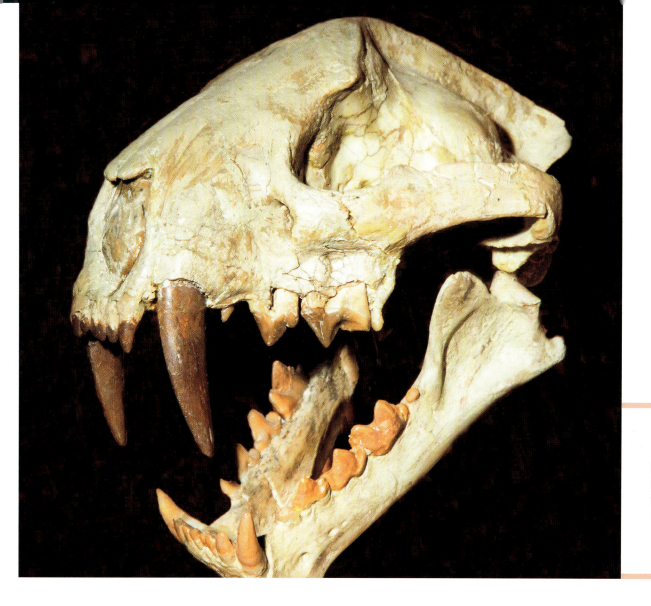

Saber-toothed cat fossils have revealed these felines' long canine teeth.

jaguar, leopard, snow leopard, and two species of clouded leopards, which actually cannot roar

because of a later adaptation in the structure of their throats.

Approximately 8 to 10 MYA, an ice age caused sea levels to drop dramatically, 200 feet (60 m) below current levels.[5] Land bridges opened up, and cats crossed the Bering Land Bridge from Asia into North America. When sea levels again rose, from 8 to 7.2 MYA, the American population was isolated. Approximately 6.7 MYA, the puma lineage diverged in the Americas. This led to the American cheetah, the jaguarundi, and the puma, also called the mountain lion.

After the puma split, sea levels dropped again and opened a land bridge into South America. There, big cats found a variety of niches and no placental carnivores. The marsupial carnivores could not compete for food or territory against the felines, and soon, many became extinct.

This is also when the cheetah moved across the Bering Land Bridge from the Americas into Asia and later into Africa. After the last ice age, the cheetahs and pumas died off in North America. Pumas continued to move. Some of those from South America repopulated North America. In Asia, snow leopards adapted to the

PSEUDAELURUS

In most ways, *Pseudaelurus* looked like a modern cat. There are some exceptions to this catlike appearance. The bones in its paws were shorter than those of modern felines, its rear legs were longer than its front legs, and its back was longer and even more flexible than that of a cat. Otherwise, whether the size of a house cat or a cougar, the approximately 12 *Pseudaelurus* species resembled their modern relatives.[6]

Today, pumas live in a variety of climates in North America, from warm to cold.

high elevations of central Asia. The question remained—as additional fossils were discovered, would they contradict or support these findings?

FOSSIL EVIDENCE

In 2010, paleontologist Jack Tseng of the American Museum of Natural History in New York City and some colleagues went out to look for fossils on the Tibetan Plateau. They stopped their SUVs to scout areas likely holding fossils. They hoped to find some bone fragments.

Then they saw a fossil sticking up out of the dirt. "It was a partial lower jaw of a carnivore, and because of the preserved roots we could get a rough tooth count," says Tseng. "That plus the overall size told us it was from a fossil cat."[7] Tseng and the others knew that cats have fewer overall teeth than other carnivores. More of these teeth are specialized for shearing meat rather than crushing bones.

TINY HUNTERS

Carlos Driscoll, a graduate student at the University of Oxford, found that all domestic cats carry genes from wildcats in Israel and the Middle East. This is probably the area in which cats first became tame. Scientists believe that as nomadic hunter-gatherers settled and began to farm, their stores of grain attracted rodents. These rodents in turn attracted wildcats, which settled near the human settlements and slowly became tame.

The group kept looking and found the bones of foxes, pikas, badgers, and various hoofed animals. They had found a fossil bed with many fossilized animals in one place. The bones had been covered, so they weren't weathered. Then they found the best part. "We uncovered the top of a skull, and I knew right away, from the width and the way the snout tapered off, it, too, was from a cat," Tseng says.[8]

The group removed the skull with a large portion of the surrounding earth and took the find back to Los Angeles for study. As they examined the skull, they realized that it was very similar to that of a snow leopard. They dated it to about 6 MYA and named it *Panthera blytheae*.

Before this find, the oldest cat fossils were 3.8 million years old and came from Africa. But this fossil discovery seemed to support O'Brien and Johnson's assertion that cats evolved in southern Asia. Tseng and other scientists suspect that there are fossils yet to find and that maybe something more will be found in and around the Tibetan Plateau.

FOSSIL SAFETY

Moving a fragile fossil is tricky business. Because of this, scientists seldom excavate a fossil down to bare bone. Instead, they remove it with the surrounding soil, which supports the fossil. While transporting a large block of earth and stone might seem unnecessary, it can mean that the scientist can study a whole fossil instead of shattered remains. Once transported to a laboratory, the soil can then be carefully removed in conditions where the fossil can be safely supported.

CLOUDED LEOPARD ADAPTATIONS

A cat's coat color isn't the only adaptation that helps it hunt. Cats as a whole have sharp canines and good senses and are very agile. But clouded leopards are treetop hunters with special adaptations for their environment. Their short legs mean they have a low center of gravity, which helps them keep their balance as they move swiftly through the trees. Their long tails also help with balance. Retractable hooked front claws help them climb, but so does another adaptation. The front-facing paws of domestic cats are great for climbing up into a tree, but they make climbing back down tricky. Clouded leopards can rotate their rear ankles much the way a person rotates a hand. Because of this, the clouded leopard can easily climb down trees head first, grasping the sides of the trunk with rotated rear feet.

HUNTING ADAPTATIONS

Adaptations occur in more than just the skeletal system and brains of various mammals. William Allen studies animal behavior at the University of Bristol's School of Experimental Psychology. He and several university colleagues studied coat color and color patterns in cats and matched them to the environment in which they hunt. Coat colors provide the camouflage that allows cats to be successful hunters either in an ambush or a long-distance run.

Cats that live in rain forests and other areas of dappled sunlight need the camouflage that irregular spots provide. These markings can be seen on Southeast Asia's clouded leopard and marbled cat as well as South America's jaguar. Although their coat patterns look striking in broad daylight, in the mixed shadow and light of the forest these combinations of dark and light help the cats blend in with their surroundings.

Cats that live and hunt in open, well-lit environments are more likely to have plainer coats with colors suited to blend in with their surroundings. Thus, the coat of the Pallas's cat matches the sandy gray of its rocky, central Asian environment. The Andean mountain cat, on the other hand, has a yellowish-gray coat that better matches the rocks and soil of the Andes Mountains. Mountain lions and lions have even plainer coats, more suited for hunting in sunny, open expanses.

Allen acknowledged that there are exceptions. The spotted cheetah hunts in African grasslands. What is the evolutionary advantage of this big cat's spots? Allen admits they don't know what role microenvironments—the environments of particular organisms, such as a particular species of cat—may have in the impact of coat coloration and patterning. But there could also be a behavioral factor that no one has yet considered. There is more work to be done.

Humpback whales are one of the many species of whales.

CHAPTER EIGHT

Whales

Whales are part of a group of animals known as cetaceans. In addition to whales, this aquatic group includes porpoises and dolphins. Cetaceans have a unique breathing adaptation well suited to their aquatic environment. Instead of breathing through nostrils located low on their faces, cetaceans pull in air through a blowhole. Located on top of the head, this modified nostril is a single opening that can be sealed to keep water out when a whale dives.

With their sleek bodies, whales closely resemble other aquatic mammals such as seals and walruses, but whales are not closely related to them. Instead, whales belong to another group, Artiodactyla. This group includes modern cows, pigs, giraffes, sheep, camels, and hippos. All artiodactyls have two things in common, starting with their toes. While horses have evolved to have only one

Whales cannot breathe through their mouths, so their blowholes are the only way for them to get air.

functional toe per foot, artiodactyls, including the earliest whale ancestors, mostly evolved two

toes per foot.

The second unique trait is in the shape of their talus, or anklebone. The anklebone occurs in other mammals, including humans. In the artiodactyl, the bone has a unique shape. This adaptation gives artiodactyl ankles greater flexibility and spring than the single pulley form seen in other four-legged mammals. The presence of this anklebone in prehistoric whales tells scientists that whales belong in this group, but it took important discoveries to figure this out.

MISUNDERSTANDING WHALE BEGINNINGS

When the first ancient whale fossil was discovered, no one realized it was a whale. The find was made in 1832 when a hill on the Arkansas property of Judge H. Bry collapsed. As the soil fell away, it exposed a series of 28 bones, some of which had sediment with small seashells clinging to their surfaces.[1] This told scientists that the massive animal had lived in

STRANGE BONES

Settlers who cleared land for farming in Alabama and Arkansas repeatedly found what they described as "round bones." These were actually whale bones, and they were so numerous that people made fireplace hearths out of them and used them to hold up fences. Others even used them as pillows. Where they were especially numerous, they were burned to get them out of the way so the field could be planted.

Visitors to the Wadi el-Hitan Fossil and Climate Change Museum in Fayoum, Egypt, can see an intact *Basilosaurus* skeleton.

أكبر حيكل كامل متصل لحوت الباسيلوسـورس
THE LARGEST INTACT SKELETON OF BASILOSAURUS ISIS WHALE

the sea. Not sure what he had discovered, Bry sent several of the bones to Dr. Richard Harlan, a

naturalist at the Philadelphia Museum.

It wasn't long before Harlan received a second package. This one was from Judge John Creagh in Alabama. While setting off explosives to clear land on his property, Creagh had found vertebrae and other fragments, which he sent to Harlan. Later, he sent an additional package that contained a skull, a jaw, ribs, and limbs. The specimens from Bry and Creagh seemed to be from the same species.

Both Creagh and Bry had measured the spinal columns of their fossil finds at more than 100 feet (30 m) in length.[2] Harlan wasn't sure what the creatures were, but he knew they had been massive. He thought the bones resembled those of the ichthyosaur and the plesiosaur, two species of extinct marine reptiles that were streamlined swimmers. Because of this, he named the creature found by Bry and Creagh *Basilosaurus*, meaning "king of the reptiles."

A few years later, another scientist was showing a different *Basilosaurus* skull to a colleague. He dropped part of it, and the bone shattered on the floor. As he swept the pieces up, he spotted the inner ear bones. Only one animal had ear bones that looked like these. That creature was the whale.

Following Darwin's 1859 publication of his theory of evolution by natural selection, scientists speculated about the ancestors of whales. Some cetacean ancestors, including the fossil dolphin *Squalodon,* had pointed teeth like a meat-eating carnivore. Because of this, paleontologists believed that whales had evolved from a meat-eating land animal, but they didn't know which one.

Anatomist William Henry Flower studied a variety of modern animals from the 1860s through the early 1890s. He proposed that the whale's ancestor was a seallike animal that moved on land with the aid of its flippers. When it entered the water, it propelled itself with its tail, like both seals and whales do. But he also noted that the skull of *Basilosaurus* was similar in many ways to that of a prehistoric ungulate—part of a group of hooved animals, such as cattle and other artiodactyls, that chew their cud. To get the nutrients out of hard-to-digest grass, they chew, swallow, regurgitate, rechew, and then reswallow partially digested food. Scientists including Flower could see similarities between whales and other mammals but weren't sure how they were related.

PUTTING THE PIECES TOGETHER

In 1966, evolutionary biologist Leigh Van Valen noted similarities between early whales and an extinct group of terrestrial mammals called mesonychids. Mesonychids were sometimes called "wolves with hooves." They had long, toothy snouts like wolves. They had become extinct

approximately 30 MYA, but the shapes of their teeth closely resembled those of modern whales. Based on Van Valen's observation, scientists worked with the idea that whales had descended from mesonychids, though they couldn't trace a direct evolutionary path between them.

In 1983, Phil Gingerich and his colleagues published a description of an animal they called *Pakicetus*. It had lived in India and Pakistan 52.5 MYA. The fossil skull had been found in river sediments bordering shallow seas. Based on similarities to the skull of a complete fossil of a different species, they explained what it looked like. The animal was the size of a wolf with the elongated head of a whale, and it had pointed teeth, an adaptation seen in animals that

WIDE-RANGING ANCESTORS

Pakicetus isn't the only whale ancestor that spent time both on land and in water. *Ambulocetus* (pictured), which lived approximately 52 MYA, was a seal-sized ambush hunter. Its head and teeth resembled those of a crocodile. It had webbed feet. Another ancestor, *Kutchicetus*, lived 46 MYA. It had an otter-like body and a head with a long snout. These animals were semiaquatic, but they probably swam much more skillfully than the earlier *Pakicetus*. *Kutchicetus* evolved to live in a wide variety of environments ranging from salty marshes to shallow seas. Still other ancestors weren't aquatic at all. *Andrewsarchus mongoliensis* lived 45 MYA in what is now the country of Mongolia. It is known by only a single fossil skull, nearly three feet (0.9 m) long with large teeth for crushing its food.[3] If not a whale ancestor, it is a cousin, another two-toed artiodactyl.

VESTIGIAL STRUCTURES

As a species changes, it may end up with parts that no longer have a use. These are called vestigial structures. Examples include the eyes of cave fish and the small legs of prehistoric whales. Until recently, scientists thought the pelvic bones buried in the muscle of living whales were also vestigial. This changed when Jim Dines, the collection manager at the Natural History Museum of Los Angeles County, and several other scientists from various institutions studied the pelvic bones of whales in 2014. In land-based mammals, the pelvis anchors to the spine and provides the socket for the leg bone so mammals can walk. Dines and other scientists wanted to know what function the bone serves in an animal that doesn't walk. Other scientists had shown the pelvis provides a base for the reproductive organs. Dines and other researchers discovered that species that mate with only a single partner have smaller pelvises. Those that mate with a variety of partners have larger pelvis bones. Dines and the other scientists determined that the pelvic bone provides the anchor required to successfully mate in the water.

eat fish. Gingerich noted that *Pakicetus* had ear bones like those of a whale and the anklebone of the artiodactyl. It was a semiaquatic link between an artiodactyl and a whale.

Gingerich made one more crucial link a few years later. He found two new *Basilosaurus* fossils in Egypt. The stone deposits in which they were found were from the middle part of the Paleogene period (66–23 MYA). Unlike previous specimens, these preserved more of the skeleton. In modern whales, which have no external hind limbs, the pelvic bones lie beneath muscle along the spine. In these two fossils, there were visible hind limbs. They were tiny, the size of a human arm, but visible. Although these legs no longer functioned to help the animal in locomotion, they had not yet been completely lost.

Then, in the late 1990s, molecular scientists analyzed the DNA sequences and the proteins that build specific molecules in a number of mammalian groups. They found the same information from multiple sources. Whales are not only closely related to artiodactyls; they are descended from them. DNA evidence had backed up what Gingerich and his team had found.

Paleontologists found even more evidence in 2001: artiodactyl traits in an actual whale fossil. Two groups of scientists found fossil whales with the anklebone intact. The whales' bones had the wide groove characteristic of artiodactyls. Scientists could now follow the steps between four-legged ancient artiodactyls and modern whales. There were still gaps in the whales' family tree, but now the basic pattern was known.

Scientists continue to find new fossils and learn from them.

CHAPTER NINE

Research Today

In recent years, paleontologists have made big strides in their understanding of mammalian evolution. Some breakthroughs occur because new scientific techniques, in fields ranging from chemistry to genetics, are developed. Others rely on new finds, such as *J. sinensis* from China and the *H. sapiens* maxilla from Misliya cave in Israel.

Scientists are also taking the fossil hunt to new places, including Antarctica. Although it is now a frozen expanse, the environment was tropical 52 MYA. Professor Jörg Pross, a paleoclimatologist at the Goethe University in Frankfurt, Germany, analyzed fossilized pollen from Antarctic core samples, which are cylinders of ice drilled from deep within Antarctica's glaciers. He discovered pollens from palm trees as well as the ancestors of today's baobab trees, which grow in Africa, Arabia, and Australia. Discoveries like these are examples of how scientists are using the Antarctic summers to hunt for fossils.

The Antarctica Peninsula Paleontology Project is headed by paleontologists from a group of US universities. During their 2016 digging season, they recovered more than 300 fossils including plants, fish, extinct marine reptiles, ancient invertebrates, prehistoric birds, and teeth from early mammals.[1] These specimens are still being identified, but until they are carefully analyzed, scientists are hesitant to discuss their finds.

DRONE PHOTOGRAPHY

A new technology being used is drone photography. In the 2010s, paleontologists in western Australia used drones to search for dinosaur footprints. Although the footprints might have been easy to see when dinosaurs left them, erosion over 130 million years softened the edges, making them harder to spot from ground level. The drone can also explore cliffs and other inaccessible areas. This may have been one of the first uses of drones to study prehistoric life, but it wasn't the last.

Drones have been used to look for Neanderthal fossils in Spain.

With the use of drone photography, even amateurs have the opportunity to make a find. A citizen science project called Fossil Finder invites fossil lovers to study drone photos of the Turkana Basin in Kenya in hopes of finding fossils. A number of early hominid fossils have been found here. Site visitors review how to identify various rocks, fossils, and stone tools. From there, they can view images in the hopes of making a discovery.

Universities are also teaching seminars on using drones. In 2017, Vrije Universiteit Brussel offered a seminar called Drones 'n Dinosaurs. The class included information on using drones for three-dimensional surveying of fossil beds.

TURKANA BOY

Discovered in the Turkana Basin in 1984, the Turkana Boy skeleton is 40 percent complete, which makes it the most complete early human skeleton ever found, even more complete than Lucy. This *H. erectus* lived about 1.6 MYA and was 8 or 9 years old when he died. Scientists know his age based on which adult teeth had come in.[2] The skeleton had a spinal curvature, which some researchers believe may have contributed to his death. In 2013, Martin Häusler, a physician and physical anthropologist at the University of Zurich, challenged this finding, saying that the ribs were incorrectly positioned and if rearranged would show no spinal deformity.

NEW EYES ON OLD FINDS

Another way to make a new discovery is to reexamine old fossils. This is what happened with the amphicyonid, or bear dog, fossils at the Field Museum in Chicago, Illinois. Paleontologist Susumu Tomiya had recently started working at the museum and was looking through some of the collections. "In one room of type specimens, the fossils used as a standard to describe their species, I stumbled across something that looked unusual," he said. "There were beautiful

Kay Behrensmeyer has been an influential paleontologist for many decades. Her important contributions include researching how fossils are formed.

jaws of a small carnivore, but the genus the specimen had been assigned to didn't seem to fit some of the features on the teeth."[3]

The teeth reminded Tomiya of those of a fox, used for crushing but also suitable for eating berries and insects. He suspected that the fossils belonged among those of early bear dogs. Working with paleontologist Jack Tseng, Tomiya analyzed CT scan images of the fossils.

The digital images revealed internal skull features that helped the scientists put the fossils with the correct genera, *Gustafsonia* and *Angelarctocyon*. The scans also showed Tomiya and

FROM TOP DOG TO EXTINCTION

The first bear dogs (pictured) lived almost 40 MYA. This diverse group spread throughout the northern continents. They evolved, steadily growing in size until, at their largest, they were up to six feet long (1.8 m) and 400 pounds (180 kg).[6] This massive predator had bulky jaws and flat teeth for crushing. Then, at around 5 MYA, before the last ice age, they disappeared. Paleontologists aren't sure what happened, but they suspect it might have been the animal's size. A big predator requires a lot of food, and if prey animals died off during a change in climate, hunting could have become too difficult.

Tseng that these species should be classified as early bear dogs. "These are some of the earliest bear dogs—they lived 38 to 37 MYA," says Tomiya.[4]

This discovery helps scientists better understand early bear dog evolution and also the diversification of canines. "Studying how the diversity of bear dogs waxed and waned over time could tell us about larger patterns in carnivore evolution," says Tomiya.[5] Because bear dogs lived when the North American climate was shifting from semitropical to a cooler, drier climate, Tomiya believes understanding them better can help scientists learn how mammals respond to climate change.

Scans can give scientists detailed views of fossils, such as this enlarged scan of a fossilized woolly mammoth hair.

SCANS

Scans of various kinds are good for more than helping scientists see inside skulls. They also make it easier to compare fossils. In 2014, Jim Dines and other scientists including Matt Dean scanned the pelvic bones from a variety of whales.

Pelvic bones are curved, which makes them hard to measure consistently to compare the length of various samples. "You could put [the bone] on a ruler, but their bones are curvy and weirdly shaped. So we would lose massive amounts of information if we did that," says Dean, an evolutionary biologist from the University of Southern California in Los Angeles and another scientist working on the project.[7]

Instead of measuring the pelvic bones by hand, Dean, Dines, and their colleagues used a laser scanner. Once three-dimensional computer models have been completed, the computer can measure the difference between one bone and another. In addition to providing more accurate and more complete information, the scans make something else possible.

Using the same laser scanner, scientists can make digital copies of fossil specimens. These copies can be used for computer analysis, printed for use in a student lab, or shared with scientists all over the world. "To me it's a more expedient way of making specimens like this that might be really rare or valuable accessible to other researchers across the world," says Dines.[8]

NEW CHEMISTRY

New techniques in chemistry have also come into play in the study of fossils. One such technique takes advantage of stable isotopes. An atom normally has the same number of neutrons as protons. For instance, a carbon atom typically has six protons and six neutrons and an atomic mass of 12. Carbon 13 is a stable carbon isotope with an extra neutron and an atomic mass of 13. Carbon 14 is an unstable isotope with two extra neutrons.[9]

Stable isotope analysis allows scientists to trace these isotopes through the food chain. As bones and teeth mineralize, they take up

DATING BONE AND FOSSILS

Unlike carbon 13, carbon 14 is an unstable isotope. It decays, or sheds extra neutrons, at a predictable rate over time. This means that a scientist can measure the carbon 14 in a bone or in plant remains to find out how long ago an animal or plant lived. This technique does not work on fossils older than 70,000 years because too much of the carbon will have decayed.[10] The age of a fossil can be found by using other techniques, including paleomagnetic dating. Periodically, the earth's magnetic field shifts, reversing direction. These reversals create patterns in minerals that contain iron. A fossil that includes magnetite, one of these minerals, can be dated by reading the patterns caused by magnetic shifts.

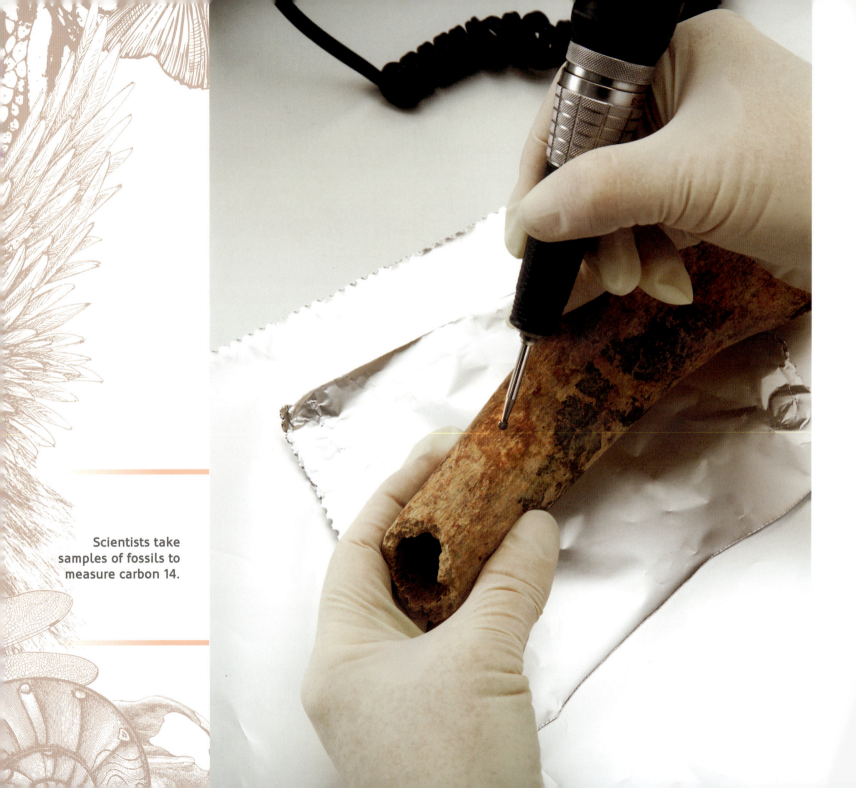

Scientists take samples of fossils to measure carbon 14.

isotopes from the water and food an organism consumes. When a creature dies, the isotopes can be measured and used to tell where an animal lived. Isotopes from different layers of tooth enamel can be used to determine changes in diet within an individual organism's life. Stable isotopes provide information on diet and habitat that can be used to double-check information gathered from characteristics of the skeleton.

Fossils are one of the oldest means of studying evolution. Using DNA analysis, computer models, stable isotope analysis, and more, scientists are creating a more accurate picture of how mammals have changed over time. As scientists continue to develop new techniques and share information, that picture will continue to evolve.

SCANNING TECHNOLOGIES

X-ray scans and CT scans make it easy to see details in bone because bone is dense. The surrounding soft tissues, including muscle, skin, and tendons, are not dense. Until recently, soft-tissue anatomy has been harder to scan because of the tissue's lack of density. Fortunately, scientists have discovered that injecting iodine into the soft tissue increases the contrast. Once iodine has been injected, the scans that can be made are highly detailed and reveal soft tissue, including soft tissue inside a living animal's skull. Some scientists are comparing the structures of modern animals with fossils using this method. They use what they learn to understand how animals evolved.

PERIOD TIMELINE

541–485.4 million years ago (MYA)	485.4–443.8 MYA	443.8–419.2 MYA	419.2–358.9 MYA	358.9–298.9 MYA	298.9–251.9 MYA
CAMBRIAN	ORDOVICIAN	SILURIAN	DEVONIAN	CARBONIFEROUS	PERMIAN

NUMBER OF SPECIES

There are more than 6,000 species of mammals. This number is subject to change as scientists describe new species and reclassify others.

IMPORTANT ANIMALS AND SPECIMENS

- The oldest placental mammal fossil is *Juramaia sinensis*. It lived 160 MYA in what is now China.

- The monotreme *Teinolophos trusleri* lived in Australia more than 100 MYA. Some scientists believe it is an ancestor to both platypuses and echidnas.

- The oldest marsupial fossil, *Sinodelphys szalayi,* was found in China. It lived alongside dinosaurs 125 MYA, was mouse sized, and climbed in trees. It is unique because the entire fossil was found.

- The oldest fossil horse, *Hyracotherium,* was discovered by English paleontologist Richard Owen.

- An *Australopithecus afarensis* fossil found in 1974 by Donald Carl Johanson and Maurice Taieb captured the public's attention. People wanted to know about ancient humans and how they lived.

- The earliest canid was *Prohesperocyon wilsoni*, which lived 36 MYA.

- All cats descended from *Pseudaelurus*, various species of which ranged in size from a house cat to a cougar but looked much like modern cats. They lived from 20 to 8 MYA.

TRIASSIC	JURASSIC	CRETACEOUS	PALEOGENE	NEOGENE	QUATERNARY
			Hyracotherium		
			Prohesperocyon wilsoni	*Australopithecus afarensis*	
	Juramaia sinensis				
	Sinodelphys szalayi	*Teinolophos trusleri*	*Pakicetus*	*Pseudaelurus*	
251.9–201.3 MYA	201.3–145 MYA	145–66 MYA	66–23 MYA	23–2.6 MYA	2.6 MYA–present

- The early whale *Pakicetus* lived in India and Pakistan 52.5 MYA. It walked on four legs but had already evolved the whale's long head.

IMPORTANT SCIENTISTS

- Joseph Leidy is sometimes called the founder of US paleontology, establishing himself in this field in the 1850s. In addition to his work with fossil horses in the western United States, he also found ancient lions, tigers, camels, and rhinoceroses.

- O. C. Marsh made a career out of searching the United States for fossils starting in the 1870s. He discovered not only fossil horses but also toothed birds, various horned animals, and dinosaurs.

- Louis Leakey is a key figure in the search for human ancestors in Africa, beginning his work at Olduvai Gorge in 1931. Members of his team, many of whom were also members of his family, found both the first *Australopithecus boisei* and *Homo habilis*.

QUOTE

"In the past, most mammal fossils from dinosaur times are isolated teeth. As a result, we know what they ate, but not how they moved. . . . We now have the first glimpses of how these mammals moved."

—Dr. Zhe-Xi Luo on the discovery of *S. szalayi*, 2003

GLOSSARY

adaptation
A change in traits within a population that is caused by different conditions in the environment.

anthropologist
A scientist who studies the origin, behavior, and development of humans.

bipedal
Having two legs.

citizen science
When regular people help make scientific discoveries.

diverge
To split into two or more species.

DNA
Deoxyribonucleic acid, the chemical that is the basis of genetics, through which various traits are passed from parent to child.

domesticate
To tame.

embryo
An animal still developing in the womb.

feral
Wild or untamed.

genetic
Having to do with genes.

hypothesis
An idea or explanation for something that is subject to scientific investigation.

isotope
A form of an element with a differing number of neutrons in its nucleus.

maxilla

The bone of the upper jaw.

molecule

The smallest unit into which a substance can be broken down that is made of two or more atoms and has all of the same properties of the original substance.

niche

A species' interaction with its habitat, such as what it feeds on, what feeds on it, and the role it plays in its ecological community.

paleontology

The study of past life, involving fossils and previous geological periods.

placenta

An organ that connects a developing fetus to a mother, providing nutrients and carrying away waste.

protein

An amino acid chain present in organic material, such as skin, hair, or blood.

soft tissue

Fat, skin, muscle, and other soft parts of the body that connect and support organs and bones.

subspecies

A group within a species that is able to breed with other members of that species but has genetic or other predefined differences from those other members.

theory

An explanation of the way things work based on a collection of current knowledge from tested hypotheses.

trait

A genetically determined and environmentally shaped characteristic.

SELECTED BIBLIOGRAPHY

Darwin, Charles. *The Variation of Animals and Plants under Domestication*. D. Appleton, 1915. *Google Books*. Accessed 26 July 2018.

Prothero, Donald R. *Evolution: What the Fossils Say and Why It Matters*. Columbia UP, 2007.

Prothero, Donald R. *The Story of Life in 25 Fossils: Tales of Intrepid Fossil Hunters and the Wonders of Evolution*. Columbia UP, 2015.

FURTHER READINGS

Frydenborg, Kay. *A Dog in the Cave: The Wolves Who Made Us Human*. Houghton Mifflin Harcourt, 2017.

King, David C. *Charles Darwin*. DK, 2007.

ONLINE RESOURCES

To learn more about the evolution of mammals, visit **abdobooklinks.com**. These links are routinely monitored and updated to provide the most current information available.

MORE INFORMATION

For more information on this subject, contact or visit the following organizations:

AMERICAN MUSEUM OF NATURAL HISTORY
Central Park West at Seventy-Ninth St.
New York, NY 10024-5192
212-769-5100
www.amnh.org

The AMNH has the largest collection of mammal fossils.

SMITHSONIAN INSTITUTION NATIONAL MUSEUM OF NATURAL HISTORY
Tenth St. and Constitution Ave. NW
Washington, DC 20560
202-633-1000
naturalhistory.si.edu

This museum contains the Hall of Human Origins, the Hall of Mammals, and the Osteology: Hall of Bones exhibit.

SOURCE NOTES

CHAPTER 1. JURASSIC MOTHER FROM CHINA

1. John Roach. "Dino-Era Mammal the 'Jurassic Mother' of Us All?" *National Geographic*, 26 Aug. 2011, news.nationalgeographic.com. Accessed 10 July 2018.

2. "Juramaia Sinensis – 160-Million-Year-Old Fossil Pushes Back Mammal Evolution." *Science 2.0*, 24 Aug. 2011, science20.com. Accessed 10 July 2018.

3. Connor J. Burgin, et al. "How Many Species of Mammals Are There?" *Journal of Mammalogy*, 1 Feb. 2018, academic.oup.com. Accessed 10 July 2018.

CHAPTER 2. MONOTREMES

1. Liz Langley. "How the Venomous, Egg-Laying Platypus Evolved." *National Geographic*, 30 July 2016, news.nationalgeographic.com. Accessed 10 July 2018.

2. "*Zaglossus Hacketti* – Extinct Giant Echidna." *Megafauna*, n.d., megafauna.com.au. Accessed 10 July 2018.

3. Heidi Ledford. "Platypus Fossil Suggests Slow Evolution." *Nature International Weekly Journal of Science*, 21 Jan. 2008, nature.com. Accessed 10 July 2018.

CHAPTER 3. MARSUPIALS

1. Paul Rincon. "Oldest Marsupial Ancestor Found." *BBC News*, 12 Dec. 2003, news.bbc.co.uk. Accessed 10 July 2018.

2. Paul David Polly. "Diprotodon." *Encyclopædia Britannica*, 2018, britannica.com. Accessed 10 July 208.

3. John Pickrell. "Fossil Factfile: Procoptodon." *Australian Geographic*, 4 Dec. 2015, australiangeographic.com.au. Accessed 10 July 2018.

4. "Animal Species: *Thylacoleo Carnifex*." *Australian Museum*, 2018, australianmuseum.net.au. Accessed 10 July 2018.

5. Bob Strauss. "150 Million Years of Marsupial Evolution." *ThoughtCo*, 20 Apr. 2017, thoughtco.com. Accessed 10 July 2018.

6. "*Thylacosmilus*." *Prehistoric Wildlife*, 2016, prehistoric-wildlife.com. Accessed 10 July 2018.

7. "The Koalas Diet & Digestion." *Australian Koala Foundation*, 2018, savethekoala.com. Accessed 10 July 2018.

CHAPTER 4. THE HORSE

1. "Othniel Charles Marsh." *Encyclopædia Britannica*, 2018, britannica.com. Accessed 10 July 2018.

2. "Dawn Horse: Fossil Equine." *Encyclopædia Britannica*, 2018, britannica.com. Accessed 10 July 2018.

3. Bob Strauss. "Mesohippus." *ThoughtCo*, 6 Mar. 2017, thoughtco.com. Accessed 10 July 2018.

4. Jason Daley. "Why Horses and Their Ilk Are the Only One-Toed Animals Still Standing." *Smithsonian*, 25 Aug. 2017, smithsonianmag.com. Accessed 10 July 2018.

CHAPTER 5. HUMAN BEINGS

1. "*Australopithecus afarensis*." *Smithsonian National Museum of Natural History*, 18 Feb. 2016, humanorigins.si.edu. Accessed 10 July 2018.

2. "DNA: Comparing Humans and Chimps." *American Museum of Natural History*, n.d., amnh.org. Accessed 10 July 2018.

3. "What Does It Mean to Be Human? Genetic Evidence." *Smithsonian National Museum of Natural History*, 10 July 2018, humanorigins.si.edu. Accessed 10 July 2018.

CHAPTER 6. DOGS

1. Alina Bradford. "Coyote Facts." *Live Science*, 25 Sept. 2017, livescience.com. Accessed 10 July 2018.

2. Alina Bradford. "Foxes: Facts & Pictures." *Live Science*, 14 Sept. 2017, livescience.com. Accessed 10 July 2018.

3. Alina Bradford. "Facts about Jackals." *Live Science*, 26 Jan. 2017, livescience.com. Accessed 10 July 2018.

4. Charles Darwin. *Works of Charles Darwin: The Variation of Animals and Plants Under Domestication in Man and Animals*. D. Appleton, 1915. 32. *Google Books*. Accessed 10 July 2018.

5. "Study Reveals Origin of Modern Dog Has a Single Geographic Origin." *Stony Brook Newsroom*, 18 July 2017, stonybrook.edu. Accessed 10 July 2018.

CHAPTER 7. CATS

1. Maryann Mott. "Cats Climb New Family Tree." *National Geographic News*, 11 Jan. 2006, news. nationalgeographic.com. Accessed 10 July 2018.

2. "Tiger." *Encyclopædia Britannica*, n.d., britannica.com. Accessed 10 July 2018.

3. "The World's Smallest Cat." *Felidae Conservation Fund*, 2016, felidaefund.org. Accessed 10 July 2018.

4. Stephen O'Brien and Warren E. Johnson. "The Evolution of Cats." *Scientific American*, July 2007. *Bio-Nica*, bio-nica.info. Accessed 10 July 2018.

5. O'Brien and Johnson, "The Evolution of Cats."

6. "*Pseudaelurus*." *Robinson Library*, 22 June 2017, robinsonlibrary.com. Accessed 10 July 2018.

7. Jennifer S. Holland. "Fossil Find Clears Up Big Cat Origins." *National Geographic*, 12 Nov. 2013, news. nationalgeographic.com. Accessed 10 July 2018.

8. Holland, "Fossil Find Clears Up Big Cat Origins."

CHAPTER 8. WHALES

1. Brian Switek. "How Did Whales Evolve?" *Smithsonian*, 1 Dec. 2010, smithsonianmag.com. Accessed 10 July 2018.

2. Switek, "How Did Whales Evolve?"

3. "Andrewsarchus, 'Superb Skull of a Gigantic Beast.'" *American Museum of Natural History*, 3 July 2013, amnh.org. Accessed 10 July 2018.

CHAPTER 9. RESEARCH TODAY

1. Michael Lucibella. "Scientists Recover an Abundance of Fossils and Geologic Data from Antarctica." *Antarctic Sun*, 25 May 2016, antarcticsun. usap.gov. Accessed 10 July 2018.

2. "KNM-WT 15,000." *Smithsonian National Museum of Natural History*, 30 Mar. 2016, humanorigins.si.edu. Accessed 10 July 2018.

3. Shaena Montanari. "Diminutive Fossil 'Bear Dogs' Reveal Early Days of Canine Evolution." *Forbes*, 11 Oct. 2016, forbes.com. Accessed 10 July 2018.

4. Kate Golembiewski. "Fossil 'Beardogs' Shed Light on Evolution of Dogs." *Field Museum*, 12 Oct. 2016, fieldmuseum.org. Accessed 10 July 2018.

5. Golembiewski, "Fossil 'Beardogs' Shed Light on Evolution of Dogs."

6. Bob Strauss. "Amphicyon." *ThoughtCo*, 6 Mar. 2017, thoughtco.com. Accessed 10 July 2018.

7. Helen Thompson. "Promiscuous Whales Make Good Use of the Their Pelvises." *Smithsonian*, 8 Sept. 2014. Accessed 10 July 2018.

8. Thompson, "Promiscuous Whales."

9. Marianne Taylor. *I Used to Know That Science: Fascinating Truths about How Animals Evolve, Plants Grow, Brains Work, Molecules Bond, and Stars Explode*. Reader's Digest, 2010. *Google Books*. Accessed 10 July 2018.

10. Daniel J. Peppe and Alan L. Deino. "Dating Rocks and Fossils Using Geologic Methods." *Nature Education Knowledge Project*, 2013, nature.com. Accessed 10 July 2018.

INDEX

ABOUT THE AUTHOR

Sue Bradford Edwards is a Missouri nonfiction author who writes about science, the social sciences, and culture. She has written and cowritten 12 other books for Abdo Publishing, including *Hidden Human Computers* with Duchess Harris, *Women in Science,* and *The Dakota Access Pipeline.*